Thai Cooking
made easy

This handy guide to the exciting world of Thai cooking features over 40 delicious and easy-to-prepare recipes—including Crispy Shrimp Cakes, Spicy Beef Soup, Grilled Lobsters with Basil, Chicken Curry and Red Rubies in Sweet Coconut Milk—all of which you can quickly whip up at home.

PERIPLUS

Contents

MAIL ORDER SOURCES

Finding the ingredients for Asian home cooking has become very simple. Most supermarkets carry staples such as soy sauce, fresh ginger and lemongrass. Almost every large metropolitan area has Asian markets serving the local population—just check your local business directory. With the Internet, exotic Asian ingredients and cooking utensils can be easily found online. The following list is a good starting point of online merchants offering a wide variety of goods and services.

http://www.asiafoods.com
http://www.geocities.com/MadisonAvenue/8074/VarorE.html
http://dmoz.org/Shopping/Food/Ethnic_and_Regional/Asian/
http://templeofthai.com/
http://www.orientalpantry.com/
http://www.zestyfoods.com/
http://www.thaigrocer.com/Merchant/index.htm
http://asianwok.com/
http://pilipinomart.com/
http://www.indiangrocerynet.com/

Thai food is one of the world's most exciting cuisines, a work of art that pleases the most discerning taste buds. Although influenced by neighboring countries, such as India and China, and later by Portuguese, Dutch, French and Japanese cooking through contact with visiting traders, Thai food has continued to evolve and gain worldwide popularity, without losing its own distinct identity.

The success of Thai cuisine lies in a blend of four basic tastes: sweet, sour, salty and spicy. These flavors are achieved by combining indigenous herbs, spices and produce: coconut milk, lemongrass, tamarind, ginger, galangal, garlic, coriander leaf (cilantro), basil, palm sugar, turmeric, cumin, shallots and spring onions. Chili, a late-comer to Thai cooking, arrived with Portuguese traders in the early 16th century and creates the spiciness that has since become a central player in Thai cuisine. Fish sauce (*nam pla*) and shrimp paste (*kapee*), which are used in nearly every recipe in Thai cooking, round out the many flavors.

The masterful blending of these four flavors is what makes Thai dishes so unique. Getting the right balance is the secret to good Thai cooking. The characteristic flavors of Thai food come as much from the methods of cooking as from the ingredients used, and the actual quantities of strong seasonings, especially fish sauce and chili, may be varied to suit your tastes.

A fair amount of preparation like cutting, mincing and grinding is required to make most Thai dishes. Vegetables and meats are cut into small pieces before being stir-fried, allowing faster cooking while retaining their crispness and fresh flavors. Smaller pieces help the coating of spices, herbs and condiments for a tastier bite. Thai cuisine is, nevertheless, not complicated to wok once the ingredients are prepared and one can be sure that the result will make the extra time worthwhile.

So experiment and have fun. The recipes in this book are mainly homestyle and require no special skill. This book promises to be your handy guide to the world of Thai cuisine.

Basic Thai Ingredients

Thai basil (*horapa*)   Lemon basil (*manglak*)   Holy basil (*kaprow*)

Three varieties of **basil** are used as a seasoning and garnish in Thai cooking. **Thai basil** (*horapa*) tastes rather like Italian sweet basil with a hint of anise and is used in red and green curries as well as salads and stir-fries. It is available year round. **Lemon basil** (*manglak*) has a lemony flavor that goes well with soups and salads, especially with Kanom Jeen curry noodles. **Holy basil** or **hot basil** (*kaprow*) has distinctive purple-reddish leaves and a mint-like zesty flavor and is used for stir-fries such as Stir-fried Beef with Basil. Holy basil is hard to find and mostly available during the midsummer months. Basil doesn't store well, so buy it just before you intend to use it. European sweet basil can be used as a substitute for all varieties if you can't find the Thai varieties.

Dried red chilies

Fresh red chilies

Bird's-eye chilies

Chilies are indispensable in Thai cooking and many different varieties are used. The large, finger-length green or red chilies are moderately hot. **Dried red chilies** of this variety are ground to make chili flakes or ground red pepper. Tiny red, green or yellowy-orange **bird's-eye chilies** are extremely hot and are used in soups, curries and sauces. They are also available dried.

Chinese celery is much smaller with thinner stems than normal Western celery, and has a very intense, parsley-like flavor. The leaves and sometimes the stems are added to soups, rice dishes and stir-fried vegetables.

Chinese pickled cabbage, also known as *tang chye*, consists of beige-brown bits of salted and seasoned cabbage leaves. These are sold in plastic or cellophane packs and are used as a flavoring, mainly for soups and noodle dishes.

Coconut cream and **coconut milk** are used in many Thai desserts and curries. While freshly pressed coconut milk has more flavor, coconut cream and milk are now widely sold in cans and packets that are quick, convenient and tasty. You can add 1 cup of water to 1 cup of canned or packaged coconut cream to obtain thick coconut milk, and 2 cups of water to 1 cup of coconut cream to obtain thin coconut milk. If you prefer to use fresh coconuts, you will first need to open the coconut by tapping firmly on the center with the blunt end of a cleaver until a crack appears. Drain the juice and continue tapping until the coconut cracks into two. Place the coconut halves in a moderate oven for 15 to 20 minutes until the flesh shrinks away from the shell. Remove the flesh from the shell, and use a vegetable peeler to shave off the outer brown skin, then grate the flesh using a blender or food processor. Fresh coconut cream is made by grating the flesh of 1 coconut (this will yield about 4 cups of grated coconut flesh), adding $1/2$ cup water, kneading a few times, then straining it with your fist, or with a muslin cloth or cheesecloth. This should yield about $1/2$ cup of coconut cream. Thick coconut milk is obtained by the same method, but the water is doubled to 1 cup and this should yield about 1 cup of thick coconut milk. Thin coconut milk is obtained by adding 1 cup of water to the already pressed coconut flesh a second time and straining again; this should yield 1 cup of thin coconut milk. You may also obtain thin coconut milk by diluting thick coconut milk with water. Many of the recipes in this book call for thick coconut milk. Consistencies vary from brand to brand, so use your judgement and dilute with water as needed.

Coriander is the most common herb used in Thai cooking. The whole plant is used—the roots, stems and leaves. **Coriander seeds** are roasted and then ground and used in curry pastes. **Coriander roots** are ground into spice pastes, while **coriander leaves** (also known as cilantro or Chinese parsley) are more often used as a garnish. For storage, wash and dry the fresh leaves before placing them in a plastic bag in the refrigerator—they will keep for 5 to 6 days.

Dried shrimp are tiny shrimp that have been dried in the sun. They come in different sizes and the really small ones have their heads and shells still attached. Available in Asian markets, they should look orangy-pink and plump; avoid any with a grayish appearance or an unpleasant smell. Dried shrimp will keep for several months. Before using, dried shrimp need to be soaked in warm water for 15 minutes to soften slightly.

Dried shrimp paste, known as *belachan* in Malaysia and Singapore, *trassi* in Indonesia and *kapee* in Thailand, is a dense mixture of fermented ground shrimp. It is sold in dried blocks and ranges from pink to blackish-brown in color. Shrimp paste should be slightly roasted before using. Traditionally, it is wrapped in banana leaves and roasted over embers for a few minutes. It may be roasted directly over a low gas flame using tongs for 30 seconds or heated in a frying-pan, wrapped in aluminium foil, for 1 to 2 minutes. Alternatively it can also be microwaved very quickly in a bowl covered with plastic for 30 seconds or so. Do not overcook the shrimp paste or it will scorch, becoming bitter and dried.

Fish sauce is indispensable in Thai cooking. Made from salted, fermented fish or shrimp and normally sold in bottles, good quality fish sauce is golden-brown in color and has a salty flavor in its pure form. It is used in almost every Thai dish, just as salt or soy sauce is used in other cuisines. Use sparingly and always look for a quality brand for a better flavor. Refrigerate after opening.

Galangal is a fragrant root belonging to the ginger family that is used in much the same way as ginger. Known as *kha* in Thailand, *laos* in Indonesia and *lengkuas* in Malaysia and Singapore, it adds a distinctive fragrance and flavor to many dishes. Though available dried or as a powder, try to purchase the fresh root, which has a much richer flavor. Fresh galangal should be peeled before using. The young, pinkish galangal is the most tender and imparts the best flavor. Fresh galangal will keep for several months if wrapped in plastic and stored in the freezer.

Kaffir lime is a small lime that has a very knobby and intensely fragrant skin, but virtually no juice. The skin or rind is often grated and added to dishes as a seasoning. The fragrant **kaffir lime leaves** are added whole to soups and curries, or finely shredded and added to salads or deep-fried fish cakes, giving a

wonderfully tangy taste to these dishes. They are available frozen or dried in Asian food stores; frozen leaves are much more flavorful than dried ones. The dried rind can be reconstituted and substituted for fresh.

Krachai or Chinese keys is a rhizome widely cultivated in Thailand. It gives a subtle spicy flavor to dishes and goes well with seafood. Fresh *krachai* is beige in color and looks like a bunch of baby carrots or turnips. Buy smooth and firm ones. Store in a paper bag in the refrigerator for up to a few weeks. Preserved *krachai* is sold in jars either whole or cut into strips.

Lemongrass is a lemon-scented stem which grows in clumps. Each plant resembles a miniature leek although the stem is quite stiff. Use only the thicker bottom part of the lemongrass stem, remove and discard the dry outer leaves and use only the tender inner part of the stem. Lemongrass is available fresh in most supermarkets.

Palm sugar is made by boiling down the sweet sap harvested from cut flower buds of various sugar or coconut palm trees. Palm sugar varies in color, consistency and sweetness, from the soft, gooey and creamy beige type which is sold in plastic

| Glass noodles (*tang hoon*) | Kway teow (rice sticks or *hofun*) | Fresh egg noodles (*bami*) | Rice vermicelli (*beehoon*) |

Thai noodles are available in many forms, and are made from either rice, wheat or mung bean flour. *Kway teow*, also known as **rice sticks** or *hofun*, are wide, flat rice-flour noodles sold fresh in Asian markets and available in dried form in packets. If fresh *kway teow* cannot be obtained, use dried rice stick noodles instead (these must be blanched for 5 to 7 minutes and drained before using). **Dried rice vermicelli** are very fine rice threads that must also be soaked before using. **Egg noodles** (*bami*) are made from wheat flour and are similar to ramen, which may be used as a substitute. **Glass noodles**, also known as cellophane noodles, *tang hoon* or bean threads, are thin transparent noodles made from mung bean flour or sweet potato flour. They are sold in dried form and must be soaked in warm water to soften before using.

jars to the crystallized hard and dark brown palm sugar sold in round disks or blocks in clear plastic or paper wrappers. The dark brown palm sugar is generally sweeter and more fragrant than the others. All can be used. If you cannot find it, substitute dark brown sugar or maple syrup. Hard palm sugar should be shaved or grated into small chunks or melted in the microwave oven to measure before using. Store palm sugar in the same way as normal sugar.

Rice vinegar is mild and faintly fragrant, and is the preferred vinegar throughout Southeast Asia. Inexpensive brands from China are usually readily available in the West (as well as in Southeast Asia). If buying a Japanese rice vinegar, make sure you do not buy what is labeled "sushi vinegar" as this has sweet rice wine, sugar and salt added. If you cannot obtain rice vinegar, use distilled white vinegar.

Sriracha sauce is a spicy prepared chili sauce sold in bottles. Made from chilies, garlic, vinegar, sugar and salt, this sauce is spicy with a sweet garlic taste and is less sour than Tobasco. Bottled Sriracha sauce is available in the Asian section of many supermarkets. Refrigerate after opening.

Thai chili paste (*nam prik pao*) is a rich chili paste made from chilies, shallots, garlic, sugar, dried shrimp, fish sauce and sometimes tamarind. A staple in Thai households, it is used as a spicy dip or added to soups and noodles. Chili paste comes in different strengths and is available in jars or plastic tubs in specialty stores.

Tamarind is a sour fruit that comes encased in a large, brown tree pod. Tamarind juice is one of the major souring agents in Thai cooking. To make tamarind juice, mix 1 tablespoon of dried tamarind pulp with 2 tablespoons of warm water to soften, then mash well and strain to remove the seeds and fibers.

Grilled Pork Satays

1 lb (500 g) pork loin, sliced into thin strips
30 bamboo skewers, soaked in water for 1 hour before using
2 tablespoons oil, for basting when grilling
Sweet Thai Chili Sauce (page 11), for dipping (optional)
Sprigs of coriander leaves (cilantro), to garnish

Marinade
2 tablespoons minced garlic
2 tablespoons crushed coriander (cilantro) roots and stems
1 tablespoon ground coriander powder
1 teaspoon ground white pepper
2 tablespoons sugar
$1/3$ cup (80 ml) thick coconut milk
1 tablespoon fish sauce

Tangy Dipping Sauce
3 tablespoons fish sauce
3 tablespoons freshly squeezed lime or lemon juice
1 tablespoon sugar
1 tablespoon minced red chili
1 tablespoon thinly sliced garlic
1 tablespoon thinly sliced shallot
1 tablespoon sliced spring onion (scallion)

1 Make the Marinade first by combining all the ingredients in a large bowl and mixing well. Add the pork strips to the Marinade, mix until well coated and marinate for at least 3 hours or overnight if possible.

2 To make the Tangy Dipping Sauce, combine all the ingredients in a serving bowl and stir until the sugar is dissolved. Dilute with 1 or 2 tablespoons of water if needed. Set aside.

3 Thread each marinated pork strip onto a bamboo skewer. Thread all the pork strips in this manner and grill, a few at a time, on a pan grill or under a preheated broiler for about 5 minutes on each side, brushing with a little oil, until cooked. Transfer to a serving platter.

4 Serve hot as a snack with a bowl of Tangy Dipping Sauce or Sweet Thai Chili Sauce (page 11) on the side, garnished with coriander leaves (cilantro), or serve as a main course with steamed rice.

Serves 4 to 6
Preparation time: 30 mins + 3 hours to marinate
Cooking time: 20 mins

Crispy Shrimp Cakes (Tod Mun Goong)

1 lb (500 g) fresh shrimp, peeled and deveined
5 oz (150 g) ground pork (optional)
$1/2$ teaspoon salt
1 tablespoon fish sauce
1 tablespoon sugar
$1/4$ teaspoon ground white pepper
1 cup (60 g) breadcrumbs
Oil for deep-frying
2 chunks fresh or canned pineapple, thinly sliced, to garnish (optional)
Chinese plum sauce, to serve (optional)

Sweet Thai Chili Sauce
2 tablespoons water
2 tablespoons fish sauce
$1/2$ cup (100 g) sugar
$1/2$ small cucumber, halved and thinly sliced to yield about $1/2$ cup
1 tablespoon minced garlic
1 teaspoon minced red chili
$1/4$ cup (60 ml) rice vinegar
4 tablespoons crushed roasted unsalted peanuts
$1/4$ teaspoon salt
Sprigs of coriander leaves (cilantro)

1 To make the Sweet Thai Chili Sauce, bring the water, fish sauce and sugar to a boil in a saucepan over medium heat, and simmer for 2 to 3 minutes, stirring constantly, until the mixture turns into a thin syrup. Remove from the heat and set aside. About 10 minutes before serving, combine all the other ingredients with the syrup and mix well. Transfer to a serving bowl.

2 Grind the peeled shrimp to a paste in a food processor. Combine the shrimp, pork (if using), salt, fish sauce, sugar and pepper in a large bowl and mix until well blended.

3 Wet your hands, spoon 1 tablespoon of the mixture and shape it into a ball, then press it flat to form a round cake. Coat the cake on all sides with the breadcrumbs. Continue until all the mixture is used up.

4 Heat the oil in a wok or saucepan until hot. Gradually lower the coated cakes into the oil, a few at a time, and deep-fry for about 5 minutes, turning occasionally, until golden brown on all sides. Remove and drain on paper towels.

5 Line a serving platter with the pineapple slices (if using) and arrange the deep-fried cakes on top. Serve hot with a bowl of Sweet Thai Chili Sauce or Chinese plum sauce (if using) on the side.

Serves 4 to 6
Preparation time: 30 mins
Cooking time: 20 mins

Spicy Steamed Fish Parcels

6 large banana leaf sheets, soaked in hot water until soft or 1 baking pan (8 x 8 in/20 x 20 cm)
Toothpicks or staples, for fastening
2 cups (500 ml) water
$^1/_4$ teaspoon salt
10 oz (300 g) Chinese cabbage, thinly sliced to yield 3 cups
1 lb (500 g) fresh white fish fillets (catfish, snapper, grouper or mackerel)
2 tablespoons fish sauce
1 cup (250 ml) thick coconut milk
1 egg, beaten
4 kaffir lime leaves, thinly sliced into fine strips

2 tablespoons cornstarch
$^1/_4$ teaspoon salt
Sprigs of coriander leaves (cilantro), to garnish

Chili Paste
5 to 8 dried red chilies, soaked in warm water until soft, stems discarded, deseeded
2 finger-length red chilies, deseeded and sliced
2 stalks lemongrass, thick bottom parts only, outer layers discarded, inner parts sliced
1 in (2$^1/_2$ cm) fresh galangal root, peeled and sliced
2 kaffir lime leaves, sliced

2 in (5 cm) *krachai* (Chinese keys) or fresh young ginger root, peeled and sliced
4 cloves garlic
6 shallots
1 teaspoon black peppercorns
1 teaspoon dried shrimp paste
1 teaspoon salt

Makes 12 parcels
Preparation time: 1 hour
Cooking time: 25 mins

1 Make the Chili Paste first by grinding all the ingredients to a smooth paste in a blender or food processor, adding some water to keep the blades turning if necessary. Transfer to a bowl and set aside.

2 Cut out twenty-four 7-in (18-cm) circles from the banana leaf sheets. To make a banana leaf cup, lay 2 circles on top of one another and fold up the edges to form a cup, fastening the folded corners with toothpicks or staples. Continue with the remaining circles to make a total of 12 cups.

3 Bring the water and salt to a boil in a pot and blanch the cabbage for 2 to 3 minutes until tender. Drain well and set aside.

4 Mince $^1/_4$ of the fish fillets and slice the remaining $^3/_4$ into thin pieces. Set aside.

5 Combine the minced fish, fish sauce and Chili Paste in a mixing bowl and mix until well blended. Add $^1/_2$ of the coconut milk, a little at a time, stirring to mix well. Add the fish pieces, egg and kaffir lime leaves, and mix until well combined.

6 Line each banana leaf cup with some cabbage and spoon the fish mixture over until $^2/_3$ full. If using a baking pan, lightly grease the pan and place all the cabbage in the pan and top with the fish mixture.

7 Combine the remaining coconut milk, cornstarch and salt in a bowl and mix well. Spread 2 tablespoons of the coconut mixture over the fish mixture in each banana leaf cup or all of the coconut mixture in the baking pan.

8 Place the fish parcels or baking pan in a steamer, cover and steam for 15 to 20 minutes until cooked. Serve hot, garnished with coriander leaves (cilantro).

Golden Cups (Kratong Thong)

Oil for deep-frying
Tartlet molds

Batter
1 1/2 cups (225 g) flour
1 egg
1/2 teaspoon salt
1 cup (250 ml) water

Filling
10 peppercorns
2 coriander (cilantro)
  roots
3 cloves garlic
2 tablespoons oil
1 skinless chicken breast,
  diced to yield about
  1/2 cup diced chicken
4 tablespoons diced onion
2 cups (10 oz/300 g) fresh
  or frozen corn kernels
2 tablespoons fish sauce
  or soy sauce
1 tablespoon sugar
Sprigs of coriander leaves
  (cilantro), to garnish
1 finger-length red chili,
  deseeded and cut into
  thin strips, to garnish

Makes 24 cups
Preparation time: **15 mins**
Cooking time: **20 mins**

1 Mix all the Batter ingredients in a bowl until a smooth batter is obtained.

2 Heat the oil in a wok or saucepan over medium heat until hot. Using tongs, briefly dip a tartlet mold in the hot oil, then dip the bottom of the mold in the Batter to coat it well on the bottom side only. Return the coated mold to the oil and deep-fry until the cup detaches from the mold and turns golden brown, 1 to 2 minutes. Remove the cup from the oil and drain on paper towels. If the cup does not detach from the mold during deep-frying, remove the mold and cup together and set aside to cool on paper towels. The cup should come loose after about 5 minutes. Repeat to make cups with the remaining Batter.

3 To make the Filling, grind the peppercorns in a mortar or blender until fine. Combine with the coriander roots and garlic, and grind to a paste. Heat the oil in a wok or skillet over medium heat and stir-fry the ground mixture until fragrant, 1 to 2 minutes. Add the chicken and stir-fry until it changes color, then add the onion and corn. Stir-fry the mixture for 3 to 4 minutes, seasoning with the fish sauce and sugar, until the mixture is cooked and well combined. Remove from the heat.

4 Spoon the Filling into the cups just before serving. Garnish each cup with coriander leaves (cilantro) and chili slices.

For an interesting variation called "golden nests", use cooked and drained rice vermicelli or egg noodles— press a small portion of the noodles into a small wire mesh basket and press the noodles into place with a mold that fits into the basket, then deep-fry until crisp.

Dip the mold into the batter to coat the bottom side of the mold only.

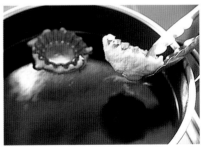

Remove from the oil when golden brown and drain on paper towels.

Hot and Sour Shrimp and Lemongrass Soup (Tom Yam Goong)

6 cups (1$^1/_2$ liters) chicken stock or 2 to 3 chicken stock cubes dissolved in 6 cups (1$^1/_2$ liters) hot water
1 lb (500 g) fresh shrimp, peeled and deveined, tails intact, shells reserved
2 stalks lemongrass, thick bottom parts only, outer layers discarded, inner parts bruised
3 slices fresh galangal root
1 tablespoon crushed coriander (cilantro) roots
3 kaffir lime leaves, torn into small pieces
5 oz (150 g) fresh or canned button mushrooms, thinly sliced to yield about 1 cup
1 medium tomato, cut into wedges
1 tablespoon Thai Chili Paste (*nam prik pao*) (page 30) or 1 tablespoon thinly sliced red chilies
3 tablespoons fish sauce
2 tablespoons tamarind juice (page 7)
3 tablespoons freshly squeezed lime or lemon juice
1 teaspoon salt
1 spring onion (scallion), sliced
Few sprigs coriander leaves (cilantro), minced

1 Boil the chicken stock and shrimp shells in a large saucepan or stockpot over medium heat for about 10 minutes. Remove from the heat and strain the stock; discard the shells.

2 Bring the clear stock, lemongrass, galangal, coriander roots and kaffir lime leaves to a boil over high heat. Reduce the heat to medium and simmer uncovered for about 5 minutes, then add the shrimp, button mushrooms and tomato, and continue to simmer until the shrimp turn pink and are just cooked, 2 to 3 minutes. Do not overcook the shrimp. Remove from the heat, stir in all the other ingredients and mix well, adjusting the seasonings by adding more fish sauce, tamarind or lime juice if desired.

3 Serve hot in individual serving bowls.

You may use sliced fish, squid and mussels in this very popular hot and sour soup. If tamarind is not available, increase the amount of lime or lemon juice to 5 tablespoons.

Serves 4 to 6
Preparation time: **20 mins**
Cooking time: **20 mins**

Coconut Chicken Soup (Tom Kha Gai)

4 cups (1 liter) chicken stock or 1 to 2 chicken stock cubes dissolved in 4 cups (1 liter) hot water
2 cups (500 ml) thick coconut milk
8 oz (250 g) boneless chicken meat, thinly sliced
1 stalk lemongrass, thick bottom part only, outer layers discarded, inner part bruised
12 thin slices fresh galangal root
3 kaffir lime leaves, torn into small pieces
2 cloves garlic, crushed
$1/2$ teaspoon salt
$1/4$ teaspoon freshly ground black pepper
8 oz (250 g) fresh mushrooms (shiitake or button mushrooms), stems discarded, caps sliced
2 tablespoons fish sauce
3 tablespoons freshly squeezed lime juice
1 spring onion (scallion), thinly sliced
Few sprigs coriander leaves (cilantro), minced
1 to 2 finger-length red chilies, sliced (optional)

1 Bring the chicken stock, $1/2$ of the coconut milk and the chicken slowly to a boil in a large saucepan or stockpot over medium heat. Add the lemongrass, galangal, kaffir lime leaves, garlic, salt and pepper, stir well and bring to a boil again. Reduce the heat to low and simmer uncovered for about 15 minutes, stirring occasionally, until the chicken is cooked.

2 Add the mushroom slices and simmer for 5 more minutes, then stir in the remaining coconut milk. Remove the soup from the heat when it is about to boil and season with the fish sauce and lime juice. Transfer to a serving bowl and top with a sprinkling of spring onion, coriander leaves (cilantro) and chili (if desired). Serve hot.

Serves 4 to 6
Preparation time: 15 mins
Cooking time: 30 mins

Rice Soup with Fish (Khao Tom Pla)

2 tablespoons oil
3 cloves garlic, minced
6 cups (1 1/2 liters) chicken stock or 2 to 3 chicken stock cubes dissolved in 6 cups (1 1/2 liters) hot water
3 slices fresh galangal root
1 tablespoon minced Chinese pickled cabbage (tang chye) (optional)
1 teaspoon salt
1/2 teaspoon ground white pepper
3 cups (600 g) cooked Thai jasmine rice (or other long grain rice)
1 lb (500 g) fresh fish fillets (red snapper, flounder or salmon), cut into bite-sized pieces
1 stalk celery, thinly sliced
2 tablespoons fish sauce
2 spring onions (scallions), thinly sliced
Few sprigs coriander leaves (cilantro), minced
1 portion Pickled Green Chilies (see below), to serve

1 Heat the oil in a wok or skillet over medium heat and stir-fry the garlic until fragrant and golden brown, 1 to 2 minutes. Set aside.

2 Bring the chicken stock to a boil in a large saucepan or stockpot over high heat. Reduce the heat to medium, add the galangal and Chinese pickled cabbage (tang chye), season with the salt and pepper, and simmer for about 7 minutes. Add the rice and bring the mixture to a boil. Add the fish pieces and simmer for about 5 minutes until cooked. Finally stir in the celery and fish sauce, and remove from the heat.

3 Serve hot in individual serving bowls, garnished with crispy fried garlic, spring onion and coriander leaves (cilantro), with the Pickled Green Chilies on the side.

Serves 4 to 6
Preparation time: 20 mins
Cooking time: 25 mins

Pickled Green Chilies

3 to 4 finger-length green chilies, deseeded and sliced
1/4 cup (60 ml) cider vinegar
1 teaspoon sugar

Combine all the ingredients in a serving bowl and mix well.

Makes 1/2 cup
Preparation time: 5 mins

Fish Soup with Tamarind and Ginger (Tom Som Pla)

1 teaspoon white peppercorns
2 shallots, sliced
3 coriander (cilantro) roots
6 cups (1^1/$_2$ liters) water
1 lb (500 g) fresh fish fillets (red snapper, sea bass or flounder), cut into bite-sized pieces
2 in (5 cm) fresh young ginger root, peeled and cut into thin shreds to yield about ^{1}/$_4$ cup
3 tablespoons fish sauce
^{1}/$_4$ cup (60 ml) tamarind juice (page 7)
3 tablespoons shaved palm sugar or dark brown sugar
1 spring onion (scallion), cut into lengths
Few sprigs coriander leaves (cilantro), minced

1 Grind the peppercorns in a mortar or blender until fine. Combine with the shallots and coriander roots and grind to a smooth paste.
2 Bring the water and ground mixture to a boil in a large saucepan or stockpot over medium heat, stirring to combine. Add the fish pieces and ginger, season with the fish sauce, tamarind juice and palm sugar, and simmer for about 5 minutes until the fish pieces are just cooked. Remove from the heat.
3 Just before serving, stir in the spring onion and coriander leaves (cilantro). Serve hot.

Serves 4 to 6
Preparation time: **20 mins**
Cooking time: **15 mins**

Tofu Soup (Kang Jyd Taohu)

7 oz (200 g) lean ground pork
1 clove garlic, minced
$^1/_2$ teaspoon salt
6 cups (1$^1/_2$ liters) chicken stock or 2 to 3 chicken stock cubes dissolved in 6 cups (1$^1/_2$ liters) hot water
2 cakes firm tofu (1 lb/ 500 g in total), cubed
1 cup (60 g) thinly sliced Chinese celery
1 tablespoon fish sauce
$^1/_2$ teaspoon sugar
$^1/_4$ teaspoon ground white pepper

2 spring onions (scallions), sliced, to garnish
Few sprigs coriander leaves (cilantro), minced, to garnish

Serves 4 to 6
Preparation time: **10 mins**
Cooking time: **15 mins**

1 Combine the pork, garlic and salt in a small bowl and mix until well blended. Set aside.
2 Bring the chicken stock to a boil in a stockpot or large saucepan over medium heat. Stir in the pork mixture and bring the mixture to a boil again. Add the tofu and celery, then season with the fish sauce, sugar and pepper. Simmer uncovered for 1 to 2 minutes before removing from the heat.
3 Serve hot, garnished with spring onion and coriander leaves (cilantro).

Spicy Beef Soup (Tom Yam Nua Tun)

1 lb (500 g) beef shank
  or stewing beef, cut into
  chunks
6 cups (1¹/₂ liters) water
1 cinnamon stick (3 in/8
  cm)
4 slices fresh galangal
  root
1 tablespoon crushed
  coriander (cilantro) roots
1 teaspoon salt
2 stalks lemongrass, thick
  bottom parts only, outer
  layers discarded, inner
  parts bruised
4 kaffir lime leaves, torn
  into small pieces

Garnishes
1 stalk celery, thinly sliced
6 lettuce leaves, sliced
2 tablespoons fish sauce
4 tablespoons freshly
  squeezed lime juice
3 bird's-eye chilies,
  deseeded
2 sprigs coriander leaves
  (cilantro), minced

Serves 4 to 6
Preparation time: **15 mins**
Cooking time: **1 hour**

1 Bring all the ingredients (except the Garnishes) to a boil in a stockpot or large saucepan over high heat, stirring to combine. Reduce the heat to low and simmer covered for about 1 hour, until the beef is tender.
2 Stir in the Garnishes and simmer for 1 to 2 more minutes and remove from the heat. Serve hot.

Spicy Lemongrass Soup with Grilled Shrimp

3 dried red chilies
2 shallots
2 cloves garlic
14 oz (400 g) fresh jumbo shrimp
6 cups (1$^1/_2$ liters) chicken stock or 2 to 3 chicken stock cubes dissolved in 6 cups (1$^1/_2$ liters) hot water
3 stalks lemongrass, thick bottom parts only, outer layers discarded, inner parts thinly sliced
4 thin slices fresh galangal root
3 kaffir lime leaves, sliced
2 teaspoons crushed coriander (cilantro) roots and stems
4 tablespoons fish sauce
2 tablespoons tamarind juice (page 7)
2 teaspoons sugar
Sprigs of coriander leaves (cilantro), minced, to garnish

1 In a wok or skillet, dry-fry the dried chilies over low heat until dark and fragrant. When cool, remove stems and deseed. Set aside.

2 In the same wok or skillet, dry-fry the shallots and garlic over low heat for 3 to 5 minutes until soft and blistered on the outside. When cool, slice the shallots and garlic. Set aside.

3 Grill the shrimp on a pan grill or under a preheated broiler using medium heat until pink on both sides. This should take about 3 to 5 minutes. Transfer to a plate and set aside.

4 Bring the chicken stock to a boil over high heat in a stockpot. Reduce the heat to medium and add the lemongrass, galangal, lime leaves, roasted dried chilies, coriander roots, roasted shallots and garlic. Simmer uncovered for about 5 minutes, stirring constantly, then add the grilled shrimp and stir in the fish sauce, tamarind juice and sugar. Mix well and remove from the heat.

5 Serve hot, garnished with coriander leaves (cilantro).

Serves 4 to 6
Preparation time: **40 mins**
Cooking time: **15 mins**

Grill the shrimp until pink on both sides.

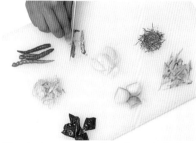
Slice the lemongrass, galangal root, kaffir lime leaves, coriander roots, shallots and garlic.

Add ingredients to the chicken stock and simmer for about 5 minutes, stirring constantly.

Add the grilled shrimp, fish sauce, tamarind juice and sugar, and mix well before serving.

Shredded Chicken Salad

1¹/₂ cups (375 ml) water
¹/₄ teaspoon salt
2 skinless chicken breasts (10 oz/300 g in total)
10 oz (300 g) cabbage, thinly sliced
¹/₂ cup (50 g) grated carrot
1 cup (40 g) fresh mint leaves, thinly sliced
3 tablespoons thinly sliced Thai basil leaves (*horapa*)
3 tablespoons crushed roasted unsalted peanuts
Sprigs of coriander leaves (cilantro)
2 tablespoons thinly sliced spring onion (scallion)
Crispy Fried Shallots (see note)

Dressing
1 tablespoon minced red chili
1 tablespoon minced garlic
2 tablespoons sugar
3 tablespoons freshly squeezed lime juice
2 tablespoons fish sauce

1 Combine the Dressing ingredients in a bowl and mix well. Set aside.
2 Bring the water and salt to a boil in a saucepan or small pot over medium heat, and poach the chicken for about 15 minutes until cooked. Remove and set aside to cool. Shred the chicken along the grain into long thin strips.
3 Combine the chicken strips, cabbage, carrot, mint and basil in a mixing bowl and gently toss to mix well, adding the Dressing a little at a time.
4 Transfer the salad to a serving platter and sprinkle the peanuts on top. Serve immediately, garnished with coriander leaves (cilantro), green onion and Crispy Fried Shallots.

*To make the **Crispy Fried Shallots**, thinly slice several shallots as desired and stir-fry in hot oil over low heat for 1 to 2 minutes, stirring constantly, until golden brown and crispy. Remove and drain on paper towels.*

Serves 4 to 6
Preparation time: **35 mins**
Cooking time: **15 mins**

Grilled Beef Salad (Yum Nua)

8 oz (250 g) lean sirloin or tenderloin, lightly grilled or pan-fried until medium done, then sliced into thin pieces
4 tablespoons fresh mint leaves
1 spring onion (scallion), minced
Few sprigs coriander leaves (cilantro), minced
1 medium onion, thinly sliced
10 lettuce leaves, torn into pieces to yield about 2 cups

Serves 4 to 6
Preparation time: **30 mins**

1 stalk celery, thinly sliced
1 small cucumber, thinly sliced
1 medium tomato, cut into wedges
2 tablespoons Roasted Rice Powder (page 68)
Thai Chili Paste (*nam prik pao*), for dipping (see below)

Dressing
3 tablespoons freshly squeezed lime or lemon juice
2 tablespoons fish sauce
1 teaspoon minced red chili
$1/2$ teaspoon salt
1 teaspoon sugar
3 cloves garlic, minced

1 Mix all the Dressing ingredients in a serving bowl and set aside.
2 Combine all the other ingredients in a large bowl and toss thoroughly to mix well. Transfer to a serving platter and serve with Thai Chili Paste (if desired) and the bowl of Dressing on the side.

Thai Chili Paste (Nam Prik Pao)

1 cup (200 g) thinly sliced red shallots, deep-fried
$1/2$ cup (100 g) thinly sliced garlic, deep-fried
$1/2$ cup (60 g) dried shrimp, rinsed and dried, deep-fried
$1/2$ cup (10 g) dried red chilies (about 10 dried chilies), deseeded, deep-fried
3 slices fresh galangal root, deep-fried

$1/4$ teaspoon shrimp paste
$1/4$ cup (45 g) palm sugar or dark brown sugar
2 tabelspoons tamarind juice (page 7)
2 tablespoons fish sauce

Makes 1 cup
Preparation time: **30 mins**
Cooking time: **15 minutes**

1 Grind the shallots, garlic, dried shrimp, chilies, galangal and shrimp paste to a smooth paste in a food processor. Transfer to a saucepan.
2 Bring the ground paste to a boil over medium heat, seasoning with the palm sugar, tamarind juice and fish sauce. Reduce the heat to low and simmer uncovered, stirring regularly, until the chili paste is thick, 3 to 5 minutes. Remove from the heat.

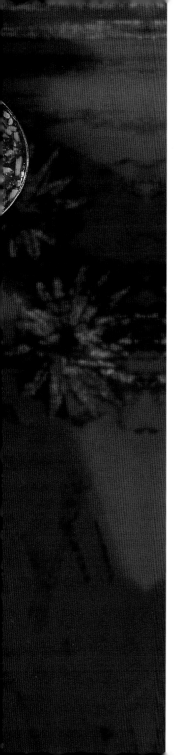

Spicy Squid Salad
(Yum Pla Muk)

1 lb (500 g) fresh medium squids, skinned and cleaned
1 cup (250 ml) water
1 small onion, cut into segments
1 small tomato, cut into wedges
1 spring onion (scallion), cut into lengths
Few sprigs coriander leaves (cilantro), minced
$^1/_2$ cup (20 g) fresh mint leaves
3 large lettuce leaves

Dressing
3 finger-length red chilies, deseeded and minced
2 cloves garlic, minced
4 tablespoons freshly squeezed lime juice
2 tablespoons fish sauce
1 teaspoon sugar
$^1/_2$ teaspoon salt
1 tablespoon Sriracha sauce (Thai hot chili sauce)

1 Rinse each squid thoroughly, detaching and discarding the head. Remove the cartilage in the center of the tentacles. Make a lengthwise cut along each body sac. Open up and rinse the inside well. Score the flesh by making diagonal criss-cross slits across the surface and slice into bite-sized pieces. This allows the squid to cook very quickly.
2 Bring the water to a boil in a saucepan over medium heat and poach the squid pieces until just cooked, 1 to 2 minutes. Do not overcook. Remove from the heat.
3 Combine the Dressing ingredients in a bowl and mix well. Set aside.
4 Combine the squid pieces, onion, tomato, spring onion, coriander (cilantro) and mint leaves in a large bowl, and toss thoroughly, adding the Dressing a little at a time, until well blended.
5 Line a serving platter with the lettuce leaves and top with the squid salad. Serve immediately.

Serves 4 to 6
Preparation time: **20 mins**
Cooking time: **2 mins**

Green Papaya Salad with Dried Shrimp (Som Tam)

1 medium green papaya (about 1¹/₂ lbs/700 g),
  peeled and thinly sliced to yield about 4 cups
1 large ripe tomato, sliced into thin sections
2 tablespoons dried shrimp, soaked in warm water for
  15 minutes to soften, drained and lightly pounded or
  ground in a blender
2 tablespoons diced fresh lime or lemon, deseeded
  with the rind
2 tablespoons ground roasted unsalted peanuts

Dressing
1 teaspoon black peppercorns
3 cloves garlic, minced
2 dried red chilies, soaked in warm water until soft,
  stems discarded, deseeded
1 tablespoon tamarind juice (page 7)
2 tablespoons freshly squeezed lime or lemon juice
3 tablespoons fish sauce
2 tablespoons shaved palm sugar or dark brown sugar

1 Prepare the Dressing first by grinding the black
peppercorns in a mortar or blender until fine, then
combine with the garlic and chilies, and grind to a
smooth paste. Mix the ground mixture with all the
other ingredients in a small saucepan and cook over
low heat, stirring constantly, until the Dressing begins
to boil, about 2 minutes. Remove from the heat and
set aside to cool.
2 In a large bowl, combine the green papaya, tomato,
dried shrimp and lime or lemon dice. Add the Dressing
and toss thoroughly until all the Dressing is absorbed.
Transfer to a serving platter and top with ground
peanuts. Serve immediately.

*A good substitute for green papaya is 5 cups of thinly
sliced cabbage mixed with 1 cup of grated carrot.*

Serves 4 to 6
Preparation time: **20 mins**
Cooking time: **2 mins**

Roast Duck and Green Mango Salad (Yum Ped Yang)

$^1/_2$ large Chinese roast duck (about 2 lbs/1 kg)
2 in (5 cm) fresh young ginger root, peeled and cut into thin shreds
6 cloves garlic, minced
1 small green mango or $^1/_2$ green apple, peeled and cut into thin shreds
3 shallots, thinly sliced
4 tablespoons ground roasted unsalted peanuts
$^1/_2$ cup (20 g) fresh mint leaves
1 spring onion (scallion), thinly sliced
1 teaspoon minced red chili
3 kaffir lime leaves, sliced

Dressing
4 tablespoons freshly squeezed lime juice
1 tablespoon palm sugar or maple sugar
2 tablespoons fish sauce

1 Remove the roast duck meat from the bone and slice into thin pieces.
2 Combine the Dressing ingredients in a small bowl and stir until the sugar is dissolved.
3 Place the roast duck pieces and all the other ingredients on a serving platter. Add the Dressing a little at a time and toss thoroughly until well blended. Serve immediately.

Chinese roast ducks (page 72) are sold at any Chinese restaurant or grocery. These are the ducks you see hanging or hooked in a glass case—they are glazed with a sweet hoisin sauce.

Serves 4 to 6
Preparation time: **20 mins**

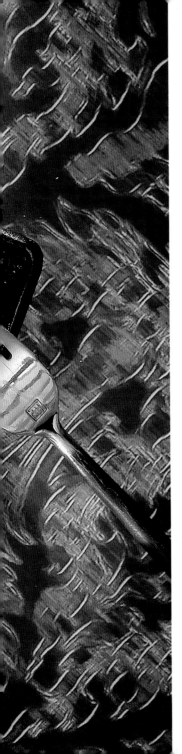

Thai Chicken Salad
(Yum Gai)

2 cups (500 ml) water
$\frac{1}{4}$ teaspoon salt
3 skinless chicken breasts (1 lb/500 g in total)
1 medium tomato, cut into wedges
1 medium red onion, sliced
1 small cucumber, thinly sliced
2 spring onions (scallions), cut into lengths
Few sprigs coriander leaves (cilantro), minced
2 tablespoons roasted unsalted peanuts (optional)
4 large lettuce leaves

Dressing
1 tablespoon sliced red chili or 1 teaspoon ground chili
3 tablespoons freshly squeezed lime juice
3 tablespoons fish sauce
1 teaspoon sugar

1 Bring the water and salt to a boil in a saucepan over medium heat and poach the chicken for about 15 minutes until cooked. Remove and set aside to cool. Shred the chicken along the grain into thin strips.
2 Combine the Dressing ingredients in a bowl and mix well.
3 In a large bowl, combine the chicken strips with the tomato, onion, cucumber slices, spring onions, coriander leaves (cilantro) and peanuts. Pour the Dressing over and toss thoroughly to mix well.
4 Line a serving platter with the lettuce leaves and top with the salad. Serve immediately.

Serves 4 to 6
Preparation time: **30 mins**
Cooking time: **15 mins**

Fragrant Glass Noodle Seafood Salad

1 small packet (2 oz/50 g) dried glass noodles
  (*tang hoon*)
8 oz (250 g) fresh shrimp, peeled and deveined
8 oz (250 g) fresh seafood (any combination of squid,
  fish, crabmeat or clams), cut into bite-sized pieces
2 tablespoons freshly squeezed lime juice
2 tablespoons fish sauce
2 tablespoons shaved palm sugar or dark brown sugar
2 bird's-eye chilies, sliced
3 cloves garlic, minced
3 spring onions (scallions), cut into lengths
5 stalks Chinese celery or Italian parsley, cut into
  lengths to yield 1 cup
8 large lettuce leaves
2 tablespoons ground roasted unsalted peanuts

1 Using a knife or kitchen shears, cut the dried glass noodles into thirds. Blanch in boiling water for about 30 seconds until tender. Drain in a colander and set aside.
2 Poach the shrimp and seafood in boiling water for about 1 minute until just cooked through, taking care not to overcook.
3 In a large bowl, combine the lime juice, fish sauce, palm sugar, chilies and garlic, and mix well. Add the glass noodles, all the seafood, spring onions and celery and toss thoroughly until all the dressing is absorbed.
4 Line a serving platter with the lettuce leaves and arrange the salad on top. Garnish with ground peanuts and serve.

Serves 4
Preparation time: **30 mins**
Cooking time: **10 mins**

Winged Bean Salad
(Yum Tua Phu)

1 lb (500 g) winged beans or green beans, thinly sliced
$^1/_2$ cup (125 ml) thick coconut milk
6 to 8 lettuce leaves
4 tablespoons Roasted Grated Coconut (see note)
4 tablespoons coarsely ground roasted unsalted peanuts
$^1/_4$ cup (20 g) Crispy Fried Shallots (page 28)

Dressing
4 tablespoons freshly squeezed lime juice
3 tablespoons palm sugar or dark brown sugar
3 tablespoons fish sauce
2 tablespoons Thai Chili Paste (*nam prik pao*) (page 30)

1 Blanch the wing beans or green beans in a pot of boiling water until tender, 30 seconds to 1 minute. Remove from the heat, pour through a strainer and rinse with cold water, then drain well. Transfer to a mixing bowl.
2 Heat the coconut milk in a saucepan over medium heat until warmed through, 1 to 2 minutes.
3 Combine the Dressing ingredients in a small bowl and stir until the sugar is dissolved. Pour the Dressing over the wing beans or green beans and toss until well combined. Transfer to a serving platter lined with the lettuce leaves, spread the warm coconut milk over the salad and top with Roasted Grated Coconut, peanuts and Crispy Fried Shallots. Serve immediately.

To make the **Roasted Grated Coconut**, dry-fry the required amount of freshly grated coconut in a skillet over low heat for about 5 minutes, stirring constantly to get an even browning. Alternatively, roast on a baking tray in an oven at 350°F (175°C) for 10 to 15 minutes. If you cannot find freshly grated coconut, replace with unsweetened dessicated coconut.

Serves 4 to 6
Preparation time: **10 mins**
Cooking time: **10 mins**

Thai Rice Salad (Khao Yam)

2 cups (7 oz/200 g)
Roasted Grated Coconut
(page 43)
2 cups (400 g) cooked
Thai jasmine rice (or
other long-grain rice)
1 cup (200 g) peeled and
crumbled pomelo or
grapefruit flesh
7 oz (200 g) green beans,
thinly sliced
1 small cucumber, cut
into thin shreds to yield
about 1 cup
2 cups (100 g) beansprouts,
tops and tails removed
$1/2$ cup (100 g) dried
shrimp, soaked in warm
water for 15 minutes to
soften, drained and
lightly pounded or
ground in a blender
2 finger-length red chilies,
deseeded and sliced
8 kaffir lime leaves, sliced
into fine shreds
2 limes or lemons,
quartered, to serve

Dressing
$1^1/_2$ cups (375 ml) water
$1/2$ cup (125 ml) fish sauce
$1/2$ cup (90 g) shaved
palm sugar or dark
brown sugar
5 shallots, thinly sliced
1 stalk lemongrass, thick
bottom part only, outer
layers discarded, inner
part bruised
1 in ($2^1/_2$ cm) fresh
galangal root, peeled
and sliced
1 tablespoon soy sauce
3 kaffir lime leaves, torn
into small pieces

Serves 6 to 8
Preparation time: **20 mins**
Cooking time: **20 mins**

1 Bring the Dressing ingredients to a boil in a saucepan over medium heat. Reduce the heat to low and simmer uncovered for 15 minutes, then remove from the heat.
2 On a serving platter, combine the Roasted Grated Coconut, rice, pomelo or grapefruit, green beans, cucumber, beansprouts, dried shrimp, chilies and kaffir lime leaves. Add the Dressing a little at a time and toss until well combined.
3 Serve the salad with the lime wedges.

Grilled Shrimp with Sweet and Sour Chili Sauce

1$^1/_2$ lbs (700 g) fresh jumbo shrimp, head trimmed,
  sliced open and deveined
$^1/_4$ teaspoon salt
$^1/_4$ teaspoon ground white pepper
Few sprigs coriander leaves (cilantro), to garnish

Sweet and Sour Chili Sauce
1 tablespoon oil
5 cloves garlic, minced
2 to 3 bird's-eye chilies, thinly sliced
1 teaspoon crushed coriander (cilantro) roots and stems
3 to 4 tablespoons white vinegar
1 tablespoon sugar
2 tablespoons shaved palm sugar or dark brown sugar
2 tablespoons fish sauce
2 tablespoons tamarind juice (page 7)
$^1/_2$ cup (125 ml) chicken stock or $^1/_4$ chicken stock
  cube dissolved in $^1/_2$ cup (125 ml) hot water

1 To make the Sweet and Sour Chili Sauce, heat the
oil in a wok or saucepan over medium heat and add
the garlic, chilies and coriander roots. Stir-fry for about
1 minute until fragrant. Add the vinegar, sugar, fish
sauce, tamarind juice and chicken stock. Mix well and
simmer for about 5 minutes. Remove from the heat
and transfer to a serving bowl.
2 Rub the salt and pepper into the shrimp. Grill on a
pan grill or under a preheated broiler using medium
heat until pink on both sides, 5 to 10 minutes. Transfer
to a serving platter.
3 Pour the Sweet and Sour Chili Sauce over the grilled
shrimp. Garnish with coriander leaves (cilantro) and
serve hot.

Serves 4
Preparation time: **15 mins**
Cooking time: **20 mins**

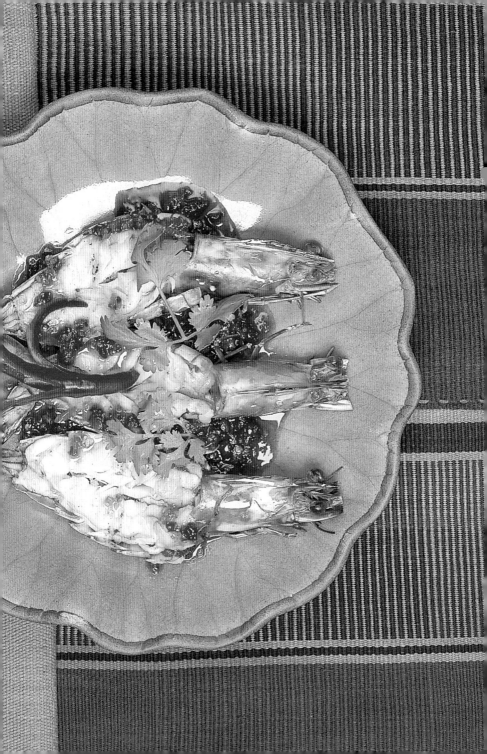

Yellow Shrimp Curry

4 cups (1 liter) chicken stock or 1 to 2 chicken stock
cubes dissolved in 4 cups (1 liter) hot water
8 oz (250 g) fresh medium shrimp (about 10), peeled
with tails intact, deveined
1 cup (5 oz/150 g) fresh or canned bamboo shoots, sliced
2 teaspoons sugar
3 tablespoons fish sauce
2 tablespoons tamarind juice (page 7)

Yellow Curry Paste
2 stalks lemongrass, thick bottom parts only, outer layers
discarded, inner parts sliced
2 in (5 cm) fresh galangal root, sliced
2 cloves garlic
4 to 5 shallots
2 dried red chilies, soaked in warm water until soft,
stems discarded, deseeded
1 tablespoon ground turmeric

1 Make the Yellow Curry Paste by grinding all the ingredients to a smooth, moist paste in a blender, adding some water to keep the blades turning if necessary.
2 Bring the chicken stock to a boil in a stockpot over high heat. Stir in the Yellow Curry Paste and mix well. Reduce the heat to medium and simmer for about 5 minutes. Add the shrimp and bamboo shoots and cook until the shrimp turn pink and are just cooked, 2 to 3 minutes. Season with the sugar, fish sauce and tamarind juice. Mix well before removing from the heat. Serve with steamed rice.

Serves 4
Preparation time: **30 mins**
Cooking time: **15 mins**

Grilled Lobsters with Basil Garlic Sauce

1 1/2 lbs (700 g) fresh lobsters, crayfish or jumbo shrimp, shelled and cleaned
1/4 teaspoon salt
1/4 teaspoon ground white pepper
Crispy Fried Basil Leaves (see note), to garnish

Basil Garlic Sauce
2 tablespoons oil
4 cloves garlic, sliced
1 to 2 bird's-eye chilies
1 to 2 finger-length red chilies, deseeded and sliced
1 tablespoon oyster sauce
1 tablespoon fish sauce
1 teaspoon sugar
10 basil leaves, sliced
1/2 teaspoon cornflour mixed with 1 table-spoon water

1 To make the Basil Garlic Sauce, heat the oil in a wok or saucepan over medium heat. Add the garlic and both types of chilies and stir-fry for 1 to 2 minutes until fragrant. Add the oyster sauce, fish sauce and basil, and stir-fry for a further minute until well blended. Add the cornflour mixture and cook for another 30 seconds until the sauce is thickened. Remove from the heat and set aside.

2 Rub the salt and pepper into the lobsters or shrimp. Grill on a pan grill or under a preheated broiler for several minutes on each side until cooked. Place on a serving platter.

3 Spread the Basil Garlic Sauce over the grilled seafood. Serve hot, garnished with Crispy Fried Basil Leaves.

*To make the **Crispy Fried Basil Leaves**, stir-fry 10 to 15 basil leaves in several tablespoons of hot oil over medium heat for 1 to 2 minutes, stirring constantly, until crispy and fragrant. Do not overcook. Remove and drain on paper towels.*

Serves 4
Preparation time: **20 mins**
Cooking time: **10 mins**

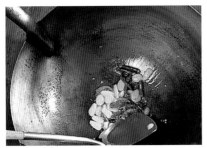

To make the Basil Garlic Sauce, heat the oil and add sliced garlic and chilies.

Season with the oyster sauce, fish sauce, sugar and basil leaves.

Grill the lobster or shrimp over medium heat on both sides until cooked.

Pour the sauce over the grilled lobster and garnish with Crispy Fried Basil Leaves.

Red Seafood Curry with Coconut

2 cups (500 ml) thick coconut milk

3 tablespoons Red Curry Paste (page 61)

2¹/₂ tablespoons fish sauce

1 tablespoon shaved palm sugar or dark brown sugar

1 lb (500 g) seafood (any combination of fish, shrimp, crabmeat or clams), shelled and cleaned, cut into bite-sized pieces

4 kaffir lime leaves, thinly sliced

2 finger-length red chilies, deseeded and sliced

1 Make the Red Curry Paste by following the recipe on page 61.

2 Next make the curry by heating ¹/₂ cup (125 ml) of the coconut milk in a wok or saucepan over medium heat until hot. Stir in 3 tablespoons of the Red Curry Paste and cook for about 2 minutes. Add the remaining coconut milk, fish sauce and palm sugar and simmer for about 3 minutes until the curry is thickened.

3 Add the seafood and half of the kaffir lime leaves. Simmer until the seafood is cooked, about 3 minutes. Adjust for seasoning, adding more fish sauce, sugar or Red Curry Paste if desired. Remove from the heat and stir in the remaining kaffir lime leaves and chilies. Serve immediately.

Serves 4
Preparation time: **45 mins**
Cooking time: **30 mins**

Fish in Fragrant Green Peppercorn Curry

2 cups (500 ml) thick coconut milk
1 lb (500 g) fresh fish fillets
1 tablespoon fish sauce
1 tablespoon shaved palm sugar or dark brown sugar
4 tablespoons green peppercorns
5 kaffir lime leaves
2 tablespoons thinly sliced *krachai* or fresh young ginger root

Curry Paste
4 to 5 dried red chilies, soaked in warm water until soft, stems discarded, deseeded
1 teaspoon coriander seeds
1 teaspoon cumin seeds
1 finger-length red chili, deseeded and sliced
2 shallots
2 cloves garlic
1 stalk lemongrass, thick bottom part only, outer layers discarded, inner part sliced

$1/2$ in (1 cm) fresh galangal root, peeled and sliced
2 kaffir lime leaves, sliced
1 tablespoon crushed coriander (cilantro) roots and stems
1 teaspoon dried shrimp paste
$1/2$ teaspoon salt
$1/4$ cup (60 ml) water

Serves 4
Preparation time: 40 mins
Cooking time: 30 mins

1 To make the Curry Paste, dry-fry the dried red chilies, coriander seeds and cumin in a wok or skillet over medium heat for about 5 minutes until fragrant, taking care not to burn. Remove from the heat and set aside to cool. Combine the roasted ingredients and all the other ingredients and grind to a smooth paste in a blender.
2 Heat $1/2$ cup (125 ml) of the coconut milk in a wok over medium heat until warmed through. Add the Curry Paste and simmer for 2 to 3 minutes, stirring from time to time, until fragrant. Add the fish and simmer for 2 to 3 minutes, basting with the curry. Add the remaining coconut milk along with the fish sauce, palm sugar, peppercorns and 3 kaffir lime leaves. Simmer for another 7 to 10 minutes until the fish is cooked and remove from the heat.
3 Very thinly slice the remaining kaffir lime leaves. Place the fish and curry in a serving dish, sprinkle the kaffir lime leaves and *krachai* or ginger on top, and serve hot with steamed rice.

Thai Sweet and Sour Shrimp

3 tablespoons oil
3 tablespoons minced garlic
1 lb (500 g) fresh medium shrimp, peeled and deveined, tails intact
8 fresh or canned water chestnuts (about 7 oz/ 200 g), peeled and diced to yield 1 cup
1 medium onion, diced to yield 1 cup
2 pieces fresh or canned pineapple, diced to yield 1 cup
1 bell pepper, deseeded and diced to yield 1$^1/_2$ cups
$^1/_2$ cup (60 g) roasted cashew nuts (optional)
Sprigs of coriander leaves (cilantro), to garnish

Sweet and Sour Sauce
2 tablespoons fish sauce
2 tablespoons oyster sauce
3 tablespoons sugar
3 tablespoons vinegar
2 tablespoons tomato ketchup
1 to 2 tablespoons chili sauce, *sambal oelek* or Sriracha sauce (optional)

1 tablespoon cornstarch
$^1/_2$ cup (125 ml) seafood stock or $^1/_4$ seafood stock cube dissolved in $^1/_2$ cup (125 ml) hot water

Serves 4 to 6
Preparation time: 50 mins
Cooking time: 8 mins

1 To make the Sweet and Sour Sauce, mix all the ingredients in a bowl until well combined. Set aside.
2 Heat the oil in a wok over medium heat. Stir-fry the garlic for 1 to 2 minutes until golden brown and fragrant. Increase the heat to high, add the shrimp and all the vegetables, and stir-fry for 2 to 3 minutes until just cooked. Add the Sweet and Sour Sauce and stir-fry for another 2 to 3 minutes until the sauce thickens and the ingredients are well coated. Finally stir in the roasted cashew nuts (if using), and remove from the heat.
3 Transfer to a serving platter, garnish with coriander leaves (cilantro) and serve hot with steamed rice.

Clams with Basil and Roasted Chili Paste

3 tablespoons oil
4 cloves garlic, minced
1¹/₂ tablespoons Red
   Curry Paste (page 61)
2 lbs (1 kg) fresh clams
2 spring onions (scallions),
   cut into lengths
4 tablespoons minced
   onion
1 tablespoon soy sauce
1 tablespoon fish sauce
1 tablespoon tamarind
   juice (page 7)
1 tablespoon sugar
¹/₂ teaspoon freshly
   ground black pepper
1 to 2 finger-length red
   chilies, deseeded and
   thinly sliced

30 basil leaves
¹/₂ cup (125 ml) chicken
   stock or ¹/₄ chicken
   stock cube dissolved in
   ¹/₂ cup (125 ml) hot
   water

Serves 4
Preparation time: 10 mins
Cooking time: 5 mins

1 Make the Red Curry Paste by following the recipe on page 61.
2 Scrub the clams, then soak and drain in a couple of changes of water to remove any sand in the clams.
3 Heat the oil in a wok over high heat. Add the garlic and Red Curry Paste and stir-fry for 30 seconds until fragrant. Add the clams and stir-fry until just open.
4 Add the rest of the ingredients and continue to stir-fry for 2 more minutes. Remove from the heat and serve hot.

Stir-fried Rice Noodles with Vegetables

4 tablespoons oil
3 cloves garlic, minced
6 oz (175 g) ground beef,
  pork or chicken
1 egg
1 cup (80 g) baby corn
1 cup (100 g) cauliflower
  florets
1 cup (100 g) asparagus,
  cut into lengths
1 cup (100 g) Chinese
  broccoli (*kailan*), cut
  into lengths
8 oz (250 g) dried rice
  stick noodles (*kway
  teow* or *hofun*),
  blanched in boiling
  water until soft and
  drained

Sauce
1 tablespoon fish sauce
1 tablespoon oyster sauce
1 teaspoon sugar
1 teaspoon black soy sauce
$1/2$ teaspoon ground white
  pepper

Serves 4
Preparation time: **10 mins**
Cooking time: **10 mins**

1 Combine all the Sauce ingredients in a bowl. Stir
until well mixed and the sugar is dissolved. Set aside.
2 Heat the oil in a wok over high heat. Add the garlic
and stir-fry for about 1 minute until fragrant. Add
the ground meat. Continue to stir-fry until the meat
changes color, then add the egg and mix well.
3 Add the vegetables and stir-fry for 2 to 3 minutes
until tender and cooked. Add the rice noodles, season
with the Sauce ingredients and stir-fry until well mixed,
2 to 3 minutes. Remove from the heat and serve hot.

Pork or Chicken with Green Beans in Red Curry

2 tablespoons oil
1 lb (500 g) fresh bone-
  less chicken or pork, cut
  into bite-sized chunks
10 oz (300 g) green
  beans, cut into lengths
  to yield 3 cups
1 cup (250 ml) chicken
  stock or $1/4$ to $1/2$ chick-
  en stock cube dissolved
  in 1 cup (250 ml) hot
  water
1 teaspoon fish sauce
1 tablespoon sugar
Kaffir lime leaves, thinly
  sliced into fine strips
$1/2$ red bell pepper,
  deseeded and thinly
  sliced
Sprigs of Thai basil leaves
  (*horapa*)

Serves 4 to 6
Preparation time: 45 mins
Cooking time: 20 mins

Red Curry Paste
5 dried red chilies, soaked
  in warm water until soft,
  stems discarded,
  deseeded
1 finger-length red chili,
  deseeded and sliced
5 shallots
2 cloves garlic
1 stalk lemongrass, thick
  bottom part only, outer
  layers discarded, inner
  part sliced
$3/4$ in (2 cm) galangal
  root, peeled and sliced
2 teaspoons crushed
  coriander roots and stems
1 kaffir lime leaf
$1/2$ teaspoon black
  peppercorns
$1/4$ teaspoon ground
  turmeric
$1/2$ teaspoon dried
  shrimp paste
$1/2$ teaspoon salt

1 To make the Red Curry Paste, grind all the ingredients to a smooth paste in a blender, adding some water to keep the blades turning if necessary. This makes about $1/2$ cup of curry paste. Any leftover paste will keep for 3 months in a sealed container in the freezer.
2 Heat the oil in a wok or skillet over medium heat and stir-fry the Red Curry Paste for 3 to 5 minutes until fragrant. Increase the heat to high, add the chicken or pork and stir-fry for 3 to 5 minutes until almost cooked. Add the green beans and stir-fry for another 3 to 5 minutes until they are tender and cooked. Add the chicken stock, fish sauce and sugar, and stir-fry for another 2 to 3 minutes before removing from the heat.
3 Transfer to a serving platter and sprinkle with kaffir lime leaves, red bell pepper strips and basil leaves. Serve hot with steamed rice.

Green Curry Chicken

1 cup (250 ml) thick coconut milk and 3 cups (750 ml) thin coconut milk

1 portion Green Curry Paste (page 64)

3 skinless chicken breasts (1 lb/500 g in total), cut into bite-sized pieces

8 kaffir lime leaves, sliced

$1\frac{1}{2}$ cups (5 oz/150 g) pea eggplants or cubed eggplant

3 to 4 finger-length red chilies, deseeded and sliced

3 tablespoons fish sauce

$1\frac{1}{2}$ tablespoons shaved palm sugar or dark brown sugar

20 Thai basil leaves (*horapa*)

1 Heat the thick coconut milk in a wok or skillet for about 2 minutes over medium heat. Stir continuously and do not allow to boil. Add the Green Curry Paste and continue stirring until the mixture is thick and fragrant. Add the chicken and $\frac{1}{3}$ of the thin coconut milk. Bring to a boil and gradually stir in the remaining thin coconut milk.

2 Add the kaffir lime leaves, eggplants and chilies (leave some chilies for garnishing). Simmer for about 10 minutes until the curry thickens. Add the fish sauce, palm sugar and basil leaves. Stir to blend thoroughly before removing from the heat.

3 Garnish with the reserved chilies and serve with steamed rice.

Serves 4
Preparation time: **30 mins**
Cooking time: **20 mins**

Heat the thick coconut milk in a wok or skillet and stir in the Green Curry Paste.

Add the chicken and one-third of the thin coconut milk. Bring to a boil.

Add all the remaining ingredients and stir well.

Add the fish sauce, palm sugar and basil. Blend thoroughly and remove from the heat.

Grilled Beef with Green Curry Sauce

1 teaspoon salt
$1/2$ teaspoon ground
  white pepper
1 lb (500 g) beef tender-
  loin or sirloin steak
$1 1/2$ cups (375 ml) thick
  coconut milk
2 tablespoons shaved
  palm sugar or dark
  brown sugar
1 tablespoon fish sauce

Green Curry Paste
1 teaspoon dried
  shrimp paste
1 tablespoon fresh green
  peppercorns or
  $1/2$ tablespoon black
  peppercorns
1 tablespoon grated kaffir
  lime peel
2 coriander (cilantro)
  roots and stems
1 stalk lemongrass, thick
  bottom part only, outer
  layers discarded, inner
  part sliced

1 in ($2 1/2$ cm) fresh
  galangal root, peeled
  and sliced
3 cloves garlic
5 shallots
2 to 3 green bird's-eye
  chilies

Serves 4
Preparation time: **30 mins**
Cooking time: **30 mins**

1 To make the Green Curry Paste, roast the dried shrimp paste over a low flame using tongs or aluminium foil (page 5). Set aside. Grind the peppercorns, lime peel, coriander roots, lemongrass and galangal in a blender or food processor until fine. Add the garlic, shallots, chilies and roasted shrimp paste, and grind further to make a smooth paste. Set aside.
2 Rub the salt and pepper into the beef. Grill or pan-fry for 5 to 10 minutes until browned on the outside but still pink and moist inside. Set aside. When cool, cut the beef into slices and arrange on a serving platter.
3 Combine the coconut milk, palm sugar and Green Curry Paste in a wok or saucepan and bring slowly to a boil over medium heat. Reduce the heat to low and simmer, stirring from time to time, until the sauce thickens. Add the fish sauce and mix well before removing from the heat.
4 Pour the curry sauce over the beef slices and serve with steamed rice.

Grind the peppercorns, lime peel, coriander roots, lemongrass and galangal until smooth.

Grill the beef until browned on the outside.

Marinated Chicken Chunks

3 boneless chicken thighs
  (about 14 oz/400 g in
  total), cut into pieces
12 pandanus leaf cups
  (see note) or 12 pieces
  tracing paper (each 6 x
  8 in/15 x 20 cm)
Oil for deep-frying

Marinade
1 teaspoon minced garlic
1 teaspoon crushed
  coriander (cilantro) roots
  and stems
1 teaspoon grated ginger
2 teaspoons shaved palm
  sugar or dark brown
  sugar
1 teaspoon sesame seeds
1 teaspoon sesame oil
1 teaspoon fish sauce
1 teaspoon soy sauce
Pinch of ground white
  pepper

Serves 4
Preparation time: 30 mins
  + 1 hour to marinate
Cooking time: 20 mins

Sesame Sauce
1 tablespoon sesame oil
2 tablespoons tamarind
  juice (page 7)
$2^1/_2$ tablespoons sugar
1 tablespoon oyster sauce
1 tablespoon fish sauce
1 teaspoon sesame
  seeds, pan-roasted for
  10 minutes over low
  gas flame

1 Pour all the ingredients for the Marinade over the chicken. Mix well and marinate for at least 1 hour.

2 To make the Sesame Sauce, bring the sesame oil, tamarind juice, sugar, oyster sauce and fish sauce to a boil in a saucepan over medium heat. Add the sesame seeds and remove from the heat. Set aside.

3 Place the marinated chicken pieces into the pandanus leaf cups (as shown in the photo) or wrap in the tracing paper to form small parcels.

4 Heat the oil in a wok over medium heat until hot. Gently lower the chicken into the hot oil and deep-fry, a few at a time, for 5 to 7 minutes each until golden brown or cooked. Remove and drain on paper towels. Serve hot with Sesame Sauce.

To make the pandanus leaf cup, cut a pandanus leaf into 10 in (25 cm) long segments, with its ridge running along the center. On one side, snip the leaf until the center into 5 equal sections, each measuring 2 in (5 cm) long. Hold the leaf with the snipped side facing down, then fold in from one end of the leaf, overlapping the snipped sections as you fold, until a 2-in (5-cm) square cup is formed. Secure the end with a toothpick or staple.

Marinate the chicken chunks for at least 1 hour (overnight is better).

Form small cups with the pandanus leaves, using toothpicks or staples to fasten the sides.

Place the marinated chicken meat pieces into the pandanus leaf cups.

Lower gently in a wire basket and deep-fry in medium hot oil until golden brown.

Spicy Pork with Mint Leaves (Laab Muu)

1 stalk lemongrass, thick bottom part only, outer layers discarded, inner part thinly sliced
3 slices fresh galangal root
2 cloves garlic, peeled
3 shallots, sliced
1 tablespoon oil
1 lb (500 g) boneless lean pork, cubed
3 tablespoons Roasted Rice Powder (see note)
1 teaspoon minced red chili
1 spring onion (scallion), minced
Few sprigs coriander leaves (cilantro), minced
$1/2$ cup (20 g) fresh mint leaves

Dressing
4 tablespoons freshly squeezed lime juice
2 tablespoons fish sauce
$1/2$ teaspoon sugar

1 Dry-fry the lemongrass, galangal, garlic and shallots in a skillet over low heat for 5 to 7 minutes until fragrant and golden brown. Remove from the heat and set aside to cool. Grind in a blender until fine.

2 Combine the Dressing ingredients in a small bowl and mix well.

3 Heat the oil in a wok or skillet over medium heat and stir-fry the pork and lemongrass mixture for 5 to 7 minutes until cooked. Remove from the heat.

4 In a large bowl, toss the cooked pork mixture with all the other ingredients and the Dressing thoroughly until well combined. Transfer to a serving platter and serve with raw vegetables and rice, as desired.

*To make the **Roasted Rice Powder**, bake the required amount of uncooked long grain or glutinous rice in a preheated oven at 250°F (120°C) or dry-fry in a skillet over low heat for about 10 minutes, stirring from time to time, until the rice turns brown. Remove and grind to a powder in a blender.*

Serves 4 to 6
Preparation time: **30 mins**
Cooking time: **10 mins**

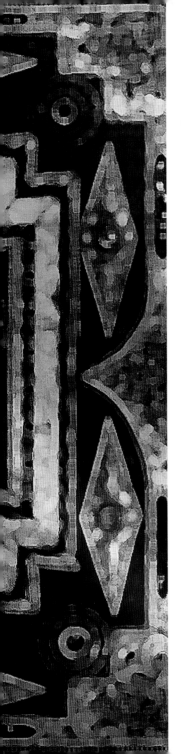

Crying Tiger Beef Steak
(Sya Rong Hai)

2 tablespoons soy sauce
1 teaspoon fish sauce
1 lb (500 g) top round or sirloin steak

Dipping Sauce
$^1/_3$ cup (80 ml) fish sauce
$^1/_3$ cup (80 ml) water
$^1/_3$ cup (80 ml) freshly squeezed lime juice
1 shallot, thinly sliced
1 tablespoon Roasted Rice Powder (page 68)
2 teaspoons ground chili
1 spring onion (scallion), thinly sliced

1 Combine the soy sauce and fish sauce in a bowl.
Place the beef in the mixture and mix until well coated.
Allow to marinate for at least 1 hour.
2 Make the Dipping Sauce by combining all the ingredients in a serving bowl and mixing well. Set aside.
3 Grill the marinated beef steak on a pan grill or under a preheated broiler for about 5 minutes on each side, basting with the marinade, until browned on the outside but still pink and moist inside. Remove and set aside to cool.
4 When cool, cut the beef into thin slices and arrange on a serving platter. Serve with a bowl of Dipping Sauce on the side.

Sya means tiger, and rong hai means crying. As one story goes, this dish was once made with such tough beef that even tigers cried while trying to eat it. Another tale says that it should be made so hot (with chilies) that tigers cry while trying to eat it.

Serves 4 to 6
Preparation time: **10 mins + 1 hour to marinate**
Cooking time: **10 mins**

Roast Duck in Red Curry

2 cups (500 ml) thin coconut milk

4 tablespoons Red Curry Paste (page 61)

2 cups (500 ml) chicken stock or $^1/_2$ to 1 chicken stock cube dissolved in 2 cups (500 ml) hot water

3 tablespoons fish sauce

3 teaspoons sugar

$1^1/_2$ cups (150 g) cubed eggplant

1 cup (125 g) seedless grapes or pineapple chunks

15 cherry tomatoes

1 finger-length red chili, deseeded and sliced

6 kaffir lime leaves, thinly sliced

10 basil leaves, sliced

10 oz (300 g) Chinese roast duck, sliced into bite-sized pieces

1 To make the curry sauce, heat $^1/_4$ cup (60 ml) of the coconut milk in a wok or pot over medium heat until hot. Add the Red Curry Paste and stir until fragrant, 2 to 3 minutes. Add the chicken stock, remaining coconut milk, fish sauce and sugar, and mix well. Add the eggplant and cook until tender, about 5 minutes. Add the grapes or pineapple chunks, tomatoes, chili, kaffir lime leaves and basil leaves. Simmer uncovered for about 3 minutes until the sauce thickens.

2 Add the roast duck to the curry. Simmer for a further minute. Remove from the heat and serve with steamed rice.

Chinese roast ducks are sold at any Chinese restaurant or grocery. These are the ducks you see hanging or hooked in a glass case——they are glazed with a sweet hoisin sauce.

Serves 4
Preparation time: **30 mins**
Cooking time: **20 mins**

This delicious curry combines Chinese roast duck with spices and fragrant herbs.

Serve family style in a casserole or pot, or in individual portions (shown at right).

Stir-fried Chicken with Cashew Nuts

2 tablespoons minced garlic
3 skinless chicken breasts (1 lb/500 g in total), cut
  into bite-sized pieces
1 medium onion, halved and thinly sliced to yield 1 cup
1 small carrot, peeled and cut into sticks to yield 1 cup
4 oz (120 g) green beans, cut into lengths to yield 1 cup
1 small bell pepper, deseeded and cut into strips to
  yield 1 cup
1 tablespoon fish sauce
2 tablespoons oyster sauce
1 tablespoon sugar
$^3/_4$ cup (95 g) roasted unsalted cashew nuts
1 spring onion (scallion), sliced

Crispy Fried Dried Chilies
3 tablespoons oil
6 dried red chilies, soaked in warm water until soft,
  stems discarded, deseeded and drained

1 Make the Crispy Fried Dried Chilies first by heating
the oil in a wok over medium heat until hot and stir-
frying the dried chilies for 1 to 2 minutes until fragrant and crispy. Remove the chilies and drain on paper
towels. Set aside.
2 In the same wok, heat the leftover oil over medium
heat and stir-fry the garlic for 1 to 2 minutes, until fragrant and golden brown. Add the chicken and stir-fry
for about 3 minutes until cooked. Add the onion, carrot,
green beans and bell pepper, and stir-fry for 3 to 5 minutes until the vegetables are tender. Season with the fish
sauce, oyster sauce and sugar. Stir-fry for 1 to 2 more
minutes and remove from the heat. Finally stir in the
Crispy Fried Dried Chilies and cashew nuts.
3 Serve hot on a serving platter, garnished with
spring onion.

Serves 4 to 6
Preparation time: 25 mins
Cooking time: **15 mins**

Fragrant Chicken Mussamun Curry

4 cups (1 liter) thin coconut milk and $1/2$ cup (125 ml) thick coconut milk
1 fresh chicken (about 2 lbs/1 kg), cut into serving pieces
3 cardamom pods
3 bay leaves
2 cinnamon sticks (each 3 in/8 cm)
3 medium potatoes, peeled and cubed
10 oz (300 g) pearl onions or 2 medium onions, sliced
$1/2$ cup (50 g) unsalted raw peanuts
3 tablespoons fish sauce
2 tablespoons shaved palm sugar or dark brown sugar
6 tablespoons tamarind juice (page 7)

Mussamun Curry Paste
3 dried red chilies, soaked in warm water until soft, stems discarded, deseeded
$3/4$ tablespoon coriander seeds
$3/4$ teaspoon cumin seeds
2 cardamom pods
$1/2$ teaspoon ground nutmeg
2 cloves
$1/2$ teaspoon ground cinnamon
$1/2$ teaspoon black peppercorns
3 shallots
2 cloves garlic
1 stalk lemongrass, thick bottom part only, outer layers discarded, inner part sliced
$1/2$ in (1 cm) fresh galangal root, peeled and sliced
5 to 6 coriander (cilantro) roots and stems
2 kaffir lime leaves
$3/4$ teaspoon dried shrimp paste
$1/2$ teaspoon salt
3 tablespoons water

Serves 6
Preparation time: **1 hour**
Cooking time: **45 mins**

1 To make the Mussamun Curry Paste, dry-fry the dried red chilies, coriander seeds, cumin, cardamom, nutmeg, cloves, cinnamon and black peppercorns in a wok or skillet over medium heat for about 5 minutes until fragrant. Combine the roasted ingredients and all the other ingredients and grind to a smooth paste in a blender.
2 Heat $1/4$ cup (60 ml) of the thin coconut milk in a wok over medium heat until hot. Stir in the Mussamun Curry Paste and simmer for 2 to 3 minutes, stirring from time to time, until fragrant.
3 Add the chicken and simmer for 2 to 3 minutes, basting with the curry. Add the remaining thin coconut milk, cardamom, bay leaves and cinnamon, mix well and bring to a boil. Reduce the heat to low and simmer for 25 to 30 minutes until the chicken is tender and cooked.
4 Increase the heat to medium, add the potatoes, onions, peanuts, fish sauce, palm sugar and tamarind juice, and simmer for about 20 minutes, stirring occasionally until the vegetables are cooked. Stir in the thick coconut milk and adjust the seasonings, adding more fish sauce, sugar and tamarind juice if desired. Simmer for another 5 to 7 minutes and remove from the heat.
5 Transfer to a serving bowl and serve hot with steamed rice.

Stir-fried Beef with Basil

4 tablespoons oil
5 bunches holy basil leaves (*kaprow*), stems removed to yield 2 cups
3 tablespoons minced garlic
4 tablespoons minced shallots
2 to 3 tablespoons minced red chilies
1 lb (500 g) beef sirloin or flank steak, thinly sliced
7 oz (200 g) green beans, cut into lengths to yield 2 cups
2 in (5 cm) fresh young ginger, peeled and cut into thin strips
1 tablespoon fish sauce
1$^1/_2$ tablespoons oyster sauce
1 teaspoon sugar
$^3/_4$ cup (95 g) roasted unsalted cashew nuts (optional)

1 Heat the oil in a wok or skillet over medium heat until hot and stir-fry $^1/_2$ of the basil leaves for 2 to 3 minutes until crispy. Remove and drain on paper towels. Set aside.

2 In the same wok, heat the leftover oil over medium heat and stir-fry the garlic, shallots and chilies for 2 to 3 minutes until fragrant. Add the beef and stir-fry for 2 to 3 minutes until just cooked. Add the green beans and ginger, and season with the fish sauce, oyster sauce and sugar. Continue to stir-fry for another 2 to 3 minutes until the green beans are tender and cooked. Stir in the remaining basil leaves and remove from the heat.

3 Transfer to a serving platter, garnish with cashew nuts (if using) and crispy fried basil leaves, and serve hot with steamed rice.

Serves 4
Preparation time: 30 mins
Cooking time: 15 mins

Fragrant Beef Panaeng Curry

2 cups (500 ml) thin coconut milk and $1/2$ cup (125 ml) thick coconut milk
$1^1/_2$ lbs (700 g) beef, cubed
4 tablespoons fish sauce
2 tablespoons shaved palm sugar or dark brown sugar
1 onion, halved and sliced
1 bell pepper, deseeded and cut into sticks
3 tablespoons ground roasted unsalted peanuts
4 kaffir lime leaves, thinly sliced into strips
Sprigs of Thai basil leaves (*horapa*)

Panaeng Curry Paste
4 dried red chilies, soaked in warm water until soft, stems discarded, deseeded
1 teaspoon coriander seeds
1 teaspoon cumin seeds
$1/2$ teaspoon black peppercorns
3 shallots
2 cloves garlic
1 stalk lemongrass, thick bottom part only, outer layers discarded, inner part sliced
$1/2$ in (1 cm) fresh galangal root, peeled and sliced

4 to 5 coriander (cilantro) roots and stems
2 kaffir lime leaves
$1/2$ teaspoon dried shrimp paste
$1/4$ teaspoon salt
1 tablespoon roasted unsalted peanuts
2 tablespoons water

Serves 6 to 8
Preparation time: **40 mins**
Cooking time: **50 mins**

1 To make the Panaeng Curry Paste, dry-fry the dried red chilies, coriander, cumin and black peppercorns in a wok or skillet over medium heat for about 5 minutes, until fragrant. Combine the roasted ingredients and all the other ingredients and grind to a smooth paste in a blender.

2 Heat $1/4$ cup (60 ml) of the thin coconut milk in a wok over medium heat until hot. Stir in the Panaeng Curry Paste and simmer for 2 to 3 minutes, stirring from time to time, until fragrant.

3 Add the beef cubes and simmer for 2 to 3 minutes, basting with the curry. Add the remaining thin coconut milk, fish sauce and palm sugar, mix well and bring to a boil. Reduce the heat to low and simmer for about 40 minutes until the curry has reduced to half and the beef is tender.

4 Increase the heat to medium, add the onion, bell pepper and thick coconut milk and simmer for 7 to 10 minutes, stirring occasionally until the vegetables are cooked. Stir in the peanuts and remove from the heat.

5 Transfer to a serving bowl and sprinkle with kaffir lime leaves and basil leaves before serving.

Bananas and Pumpkin in Sweet Coconut Milk

4 cups (1 liter) thin coconut milk and $^1/_2$ cup (125 ml) thick coconut milk

7 oz (200 g) pumpkin or yam or sweet potatoes, peeled and cubed

5 large bananas or 12 baby bananas, peeled and halved lengthwise

$^1/_2$ cup (90 g) shaved palm sugar or dark brown sugar

1 teaspoon salt

1 teaspoon pandanus or vanilla essence

1 In a saucepan, bring the thin coconut milk slowly to a boil over medium heat. Add the pumpkin, yam or sweet potatoes and simmer uncovered for about 5 minutes until soft, then add the bananas and simmer for 3 more minutes. Stir in the palm sugar, salt and pandanus or vanilla essence, and mix until the sugar is completely dissolved. Simmer for 5 minutes and remove from the heat.

2 Add the thick coconut milk and mix until well combined. Serve hot or cold in individual serving bowls.

Serves 4
Preparation time: **10 mins**
Cooking time: **15 mins**

Steamed Custard in a Pumpkin

1 small pumpkin (about
  2 lbs/1 kg) or 3 butternut squash
3 tablespoons shaved
  palm sugar or dark
  brown sugar
$1/4$ teaspoon pandanus
  or vanilla essence
$1/4$ cup (60 ml) thick
  coconut milk
1 tablespoon cornstarch
Pinch of salt
3 eggs, beaten

Serves 4 to 6
Preparation time: **30 mins**
Cooking time: **40 mins**

1 Carefully cut out a 4-in (10-cm) section around the stem of the pumpkin or a smaller section on top of each butternut squash to form a "lid", then scoop out the seeds.

2 Heat the palm sugar, pandanus essence and coconut milk in a saucepan over medium heat, stirring constantly until the sugar is dissolved. Add the cornstarch and salt and mix until well blended; do not allow to boil. Reduce the heat to low, add the eggs and stir continuously for about 5 minutes until a smooth mixture is obtained, taking care not to scorch the bottom. Remove from the heat and pour into the pumpkin or squash.

3 Replace the "lid" and steam for 30 minutes until the custard is set. Remove and set aside to cool.

4 Slice the pumpkin or squash into wedges and serve warm or chilled with ice cream if desired.

Fresh Mango Custard Tarts

12 tartlet molds (each 2 in/5 cm in diameter) or small cupcake molds
Whipped cream, for topping (optional)
$1/2$ cup (50 g) grated coconut, dry-roasted (optional)

Pastry
1 cup (150 g) flour
$1/4$ cup (50 g) sugar
$1/2$ cup (125 ml) melted butter or shortening
$1/2$ egg, beaten
2 tablespoons thick coconut milk
1 teaspoon pandanus, vanilla, jasmine or rose essence

Filling
2 large or 3 medium ripe mangoes (about 1 lb/ 500 g in total), peeled, sliced
$1/2$ cup (100 g) sugar
1 cup (250) thick coconut milk
$1/2$ cup (60 g) roasted unsalted cashew nuts, halved (optional)
$2^1/2$ eggs, beaten
$1/2$ teaspoon grated ginger
$1/2$ teaspoon cinnamon

1 Make the Pastry by combining all the ingredients in a mixing bowl and mixing well. Flour your hands and knead the mixture to a smooth dough on a floured surface. Using a rolling pin, roll the dough to a thin sheet, $1/8$ in (3 mm) thick. From the dough sheet, cut out circles large enough to line the tartlet or cupcake molds. Flour each mold and line with a dough circle.
2 Preheat the oven to 420°F (210°C).
3 To make the Filling, process the mango slices to a puree in a blender. Whisk the sugar and coconut milk in a mixing bowl until the sugar is dissolved. Stir in the mango puree and cashew nuts, then add the eggs, ginger and cinnamon, and beat to mix well.
4 Spoon the Filling into each tartlet pan until almost full. Bake in the oven at 420°F (210°C) for about 10 minutes, then reduce the heat to 300°F (150°C) and bake for another 20 to 25 minutes, until the custard is set. Remove and set aside to cool.
5 Chill in the refrigerator for about 30 minutes. Top each tart with some whipped cream and garnish with grated coconut (if desired). Serve warm or at room temperature.

To save time, you may use readymade pie crust or filo pastry instead of making your own pastry.

Serves 6
Preparation time: 30 **mins** + 30 **mins chilling**
Cooking time: 25 **mins**

Red Rubies in Sweet Coconut Milk

12 fresh or canned water chestnuts (about 12 oz/350 g), peeled and diced to yield 1^1/$_2$ cups
1 teaspoon red food coloring
2 cups (500 ml) water
^{1}/$_2$ cup (60 g) cornstarch
Crushed ice, to serve
Mixed fresh or canned tropical fruits (jackfruit, longans and lychees), diced to yield 2 cups (optional)

Sweet Coconut Milk

1 cup (200 g) sugar
^{1}/$_2$ cup (125 ml) water
^{1}/$_2$ cup (125 ml) thick coconut milk
1 teaspoon jasmine, pandanus or vanilla essence

Serves 6
Preparation time: 30 mins
 + 2 hours soaking
Cooking time: 20 mins

1 To make the Sweet Coconut Milk, boil the sugar and water in a saucepan over medium heat for about 5 minutes, stirring constantly, until the sugar is dissolved and a thick syrup is obtained. Remove from the heat and set aside to cool. Add the coconut milk and fragrant essence, and mix well. Set aside.

2 Place the water chestnut dice in a bowl and sprinkle with the red food coloring, creating light and dark red spots that resemble the look of rubies or pomegranate seeds. Soak the red water chestnut dice in 2 cups (500 ml) of water for at least 2 hours. Remove and drain.

3 Roll the red water chestnut dice in the cornstarch until coated on all sides, then place in a sieve and shake off excess cornstarch. Set aside.

4 Bring a pot of water to a boil. In small batches, drop the coated water chestnut dice into the pot, stirring gently to separate, and simmer for 2 to 3 minutes until they float to the surface. Remove with a slotted spoon or wire mesh and plunge into cold water for about 1 minute. Drain and set aside. Continue until all the "red rubies" are cooked.

5 To serve, place some crushed ice in a dessert bowl and top with 3 tablespoons of the water chestnut rubies and 2 tablespoons of mixed tropical fruits (if using). Spoon 4 tablespoons of the Sweet Coconut Milk on top.